TESOL Support

for Every Day

from

SURVIVING

to THRIVING

in the

English-speaking

Classroom:

General curriculum support for speakers of other languages

Book 2

Jenny Pyatt

essential
resources

Title:	From Surviving to Thriving
	in the English-speaking Classroom Book 2
Author:	Jenny Pyatt
Editor:	Tanya Tremewan
Book Code:	0130
ISBN:	1-877300-19-5
Published:	2002
Publisher:	Essential Resources Educational Publishers Limited

New Zealand Office:	**Australian Office:**
PO Box 5036	PO Box 90
Invercargill	Oak Flats, NSW 2529
ph: 0800 087 376	ph: 1800 005 068
fax: 0800 937 825	fax: 1800 981 213

Websites:	www.essentialresources.co.nz
	www.essentialresources.com.au

About the author:

Jenny Pyatt's experience of teaching in east and south Auckland schools during the 1990s, when there was a surge of new immigrants to New Zealand, sparked her interest in teaching English to speakers of other languages and the needs of the children in this group.

Now semi-retired and living on a lifestyle block in Hawkes Bay with a huge garden, she has combined her interests in writing and helping these students to produce this series.

Contents

Introduction

This book is part of the *TESOL Support for Every Day* series aimed at meeting the needs of students with language backgrounds other than English. These students may have been at school for six months, or one or even two years. Although they may be in an English-speaking country, communicating quite well in English and gaining confidence in their written and oral language, they have specific language needs. A typical running record in reading shows a high level of accuracy but a very low self-correction rate and low comprehension. Written work shows confusion with tenses, singular and plural, word endings and final consonants, as well as incorrect sentence patterns.

Subject-specific language must be a nightmare for these children. Imagine sitting in a maths lesson and hearing words like **parallel**, **polygon**, **circumference** and **percentage** when you are still struggling to put a sentence together. With the activities in *From surviving to thriving in the English-speaking classroom* you can build their confidence in dealing with a range of areas of the curriculum.

This book is divided into three parts. Part 1 contains short extracts of text with pictures. The children read the text, undertake activities related to the text and then read the text again, this time without pictures. If the child cannot understand the instructions, you might ask an older child with the same first language to explain them. The activities in part 2 address specific language needs. Finally, part 3 provides mini-focus language packs, which contain topics and ideas to extend vocabulary. To improve language structure, you might consider supplementing these activities with some of the many other English texts available, particularly for homework activities.

If you are assisted by teacher aides, parent helpers or peer tutors, *From surviving to thriving in the English-speaking classroom* offers an ideal resource for them to work with. A capital H at the top right hand corner of an activity indicates that a helper is required for most if not all students. Students may need assistance with other activities, depending on their level of confidence and ability.

One small step at a time

The following classroom and environmental strategies are suggested to develop the confidence of students who are learning English as speakers of other languages (ESOL) and to lead them towards greater independence.

- Provide texts with tapes for the children to listen to at school and at home.

- Collect any games that emphasise oral language, such as Guess Who? Make these games available for the children to use in spare time and for ESOL students to use with teacher aides or any other classroom helpers. Play Memory with classroom items like scissors, a ruler and dictionary, or with kitchen utensils such as a grater, items of cutlery, plate, cup and saucer.

- Some schools have ethnic boxes in which teachers and students collect pictures, maps and bilingual dictionaries to use as a springboard for talking and writing and as a self-access resource.

- It is important to encourage and maintain strength in the child's first language as competence in this area facilitates second language learning.

- Bring readers from other ethnic groups to the classroom. Children can bring readers in their first language.

- New learners of English need plenty of variety as well as interesting repetition.

- They need visual, concrete and experiential support in their day-to-day learning.

- Put together mini-focus language packs on topics like weather, school, food and sports. The children can work on them with parent helpers or peer tutors.

- Use the students who are strong in their first language to help teach their peers and to act as interpreters. Train them to welcome visitors and run orientation programmes. They can make school announcements in their first language. Target their talents and make them an important part of your school.

- Do you have someone in your school community who could write bilingual homework sheets for you? They can introduce survival questions like "What school do you go to? What is your name? Where do you live?", and cover colours, shapes and counting.

- Write instructions in homework books like "Read this book at home and bring it back to school tomorrow". New immigrant families will find someone to interpret for them, as such contacts are essential to survive in a new country.

- Write instructions for classroom tasks on the blackboard as well as giving them orally. In this way you give the new learner of English time to process the information.

Part 1

Working with stories

STORY: THE LIBRARY

Vocabulary

library

librarian

books

library card

computer

aliens

sharks

spiders

dinosaur

Reading

Read this story.

Sometimes I go to the to get some

to read. There are a lot of at the  .

There are about and about

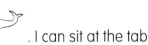 . There are about and

about . I can sit at the table and read.

The helps me to find that I like. I

look for the on the computer. I show her my

library card and then I take the books home to read.

There are a lot of books at the library .

Ending with -ing

Write *ing* on the line.

go_____   help_____   read_____   look_____

Write the correct word in the space. Choose from the words above.

1. I am _____ to the library.

2. The librarian is _____ me.

3. I am _____ for a book on the computer.

4. I am _____ a book about dinosaurs.

is or are

- Use *is* when you are talking about one thing.
- Use *are* when you are talking about more than one thing.

Write *is* or *are* on the line.

1. Here _____ a book about sharks.

2. Here _____ some books about aliens.

3. The librarian _____ helping me.

4. Where _____ my library card?

5. The books about spiders _____ over there.

6. There _____ a lot of books in the library.

Matching

Draw a line from the picture to the word.

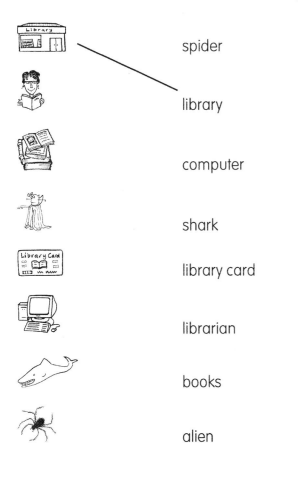

spider

library

computer

shark

library card

librarian

books

alien

Reading again

Read the story without any pictures.

THE LIBRARY

Sometimes I go to the library to get some books to read. There are a lot of books at the library. There are books about dinosaurs and books about aliens. There are books about spiders and books about sharks. I can sit at the table and read.

The librarian helps me to find books that I like. I look for the books on the computer. I show her my library card and then I take the books home to read.

There are a lot of books at the library.

STORY 2: GOING CAMPING

Vocabulary

tent

sleeping bags

swim

sea

car

food

fire

sausages

beach

Reading

Read this story.

We put the ⛺ in the 🚗. We put our 🛌

in the 🚗. Dad packed some 🧺.

Mum drove to the 🌊.

Dad put up the ⛺ and we had a 🏊

in the 〰️. I made a 🔥 and we cooked

🌭. We slept in the ⛺.

In the morning we took down the ⛺. We

rolled up our 🛌 and put them in the 🚗.

Dad drove us home.

Naming words and adding -s

Write the word on the line.

_____   

Write the story in the correct order. What happened first?

1.　Dad drove us home.

2.　Dad packed some food.

3.　We cooked sausages.

4.　I made a fire.

5.　Dad put up the tent.

1.　_____

2.　_____

3.　_____

4.　_____

5.　_____

Reading again

Read the story without any pictures.

GOING CAMPING

We put the tent in the car. We put our sleeping bags in the car. Dad packed some food.

Mum drove to the beach.

Dad put up the tent and we had a swim in the sea. I made a fire and we cooked sausages. We slept in the tent.

In the morning we took down the tent. We rolled up our sleeping bags and put them in the car.

Dad drove us home.

The child will need a helper to read the instructions and to help with any words that he or she doesn't understand.

1. Draw a line across the middle of the box.

2. The top half of the box is the sea.

3. The bottom half of the box is the beach.

4. Draw a tent on the beach.

5. Draw a fire beside the tent. Someone is cooking sausages on the fire.

6. Draw two people swimming in the water.

STORY 3: THE LETTER

friend

letter

envelope

stamp

paper

pen

mailbox

boy

write

friends

Reading

Read this story.

My lives a long way away.

"Why don't you write him a letter?" asked Mum.

I got some paper and a pen and started to write.

Here is my letter.

> Dear Toby,
>
> I like my new school but I don't have many friends
>
> yet. Please write to me and tell me what you
>
> have been doing. Your friend,
>
> Matthew

I put the letter into an envelope. I put a stamp on the envelope and

walked to the mailbox at the end of our street. I posted my letter and

walked home.

A boy from my school was at my house.

"A new friend has come to play with you", said Mum.

Draw a line from the word to the picture.

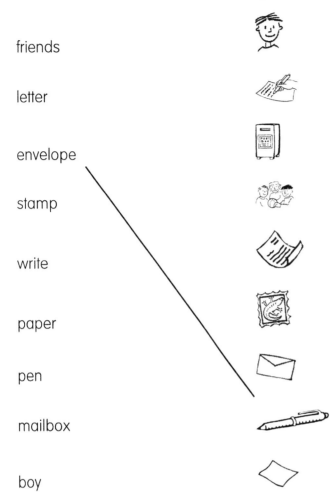

friends

letter

envelope

stamp

write

paper

pen

mailbox

boy

Contractions

- *don't* means *do not*
- *isn't* means *is not*
- *won't* means *will not*

- *haven't* means *have not*
- *can't* means *cannot*

Can you finish the sentences?

1. I don't want to _____

2. I haven't got time to _____

3. My friend isn't_____

4. Mum said I can't _____

5. We won't be going _____

Asking questions

This is a question mark   **?**
Questions can begin with:

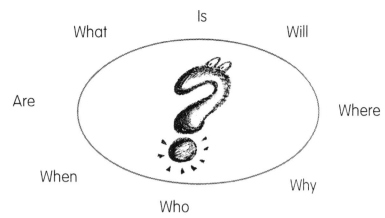

What   Is   Will

Are   Where

When   Why

Who

Put a question mark in the box.

1. Why don't you write him a letter ☐

2. What is your name ☐

3. Is it going to rain today ☐

4. Are there any pencils on your table ☐

Write a question that begins with:

1. Where _____

2. Will _____

3. When _____

Ending with a full stop

Put a full stop in the box.

1. I like my new school ☐

2. My friend lives a long way away ☐

3. Please tell me what you have been doing ☐

4. I put a stamp on the envelope ☐

5. I walked to the mailbox ☐

6. A new friend came to my house ☐

13

Put a full stop or a question mark in the box.

1. Where do you live ☐

2. I wrote a letter ☐

3. Will you play with me ☐

4. Is there a dog at your house ☐

5. At school we read books ☐

6. I take my lunch to school ☐

Reading again

Read the story without any pictures.

THE LETTER

My friend lives a long way away.

"Why don't you write him a letter?" asked Mum.

I got some paper and a pen and started to write.

Here is my letter.

> Dear Toby,
>
> I like my new school but I don't have many friends yet. Please write to me and tell me what you have been doing.
>
> Your friend,
>
> Matthew

I put the letter into an envelope. I put a stamp on the envelope and walked to the mailbox at the end of our street. I posted my letter and walked home.

A boy from my school was at my house.

"A new friend has come to play with you", said Mum.

STORY 4: GOING TO THE FARM

Vocabulary

tractor

hay

hayshed

nine o'clock

cows

pigs

horse

sheep

farmer

paddock

gate

rope

town

meat

wool

car

pig sty

Reading

Read this story.

On Saturday morning Dad came into my bedroom.

"Get out of bed and put on some old clothes", said Dad. "We are

going to visit a farm."

At we got in the and drove to the farm.

We went through the  and the came out to meet us.

First we walked into a and looked at the . They were in

a .

"Sometimes the  are out in the ", said the  "but they

come back into the for food."

We walked through the into another . There were some

and a in the .

"We get and from the ", said the , "but

the is a friend. Would you like to have a ride on him?"

"Yes please", I said quickly.

The lifted me on to the . He led the with a

I sat on the and I climbed up on the in the . We

put some on the back of the and fed the to the

.

It was a good day. We went home at

Choosing the word

climbed	rode	sat	fed	went	walked	looked

Choose the word from the box to write in the space.

1. I _____ at the pigs.

2. I _____ up on the hay.

3. I _____ through the gate.

4. I _____ on the horse.

5. I _____ on the tractor.

6. I _____ hay to the cows.

7. We _____ to a farm.

was or were

Write *was* or *were* on the line.

1. There _____ pigs in the pig sty.

2. There _____ a tractor on the farm.

3. There _____ cows in the paddock.

4. There _____ a horse for me to ride on.

5. There _____ a lot of animals on the farm.

Naming

Write the word for the picture on the line.

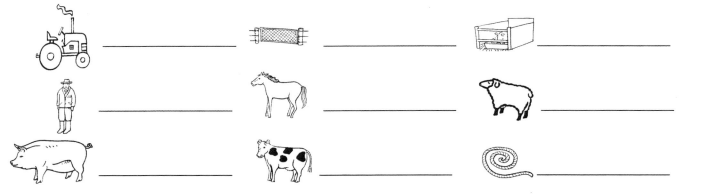

The child will need a helper to read the instructions and to help with any words that he or she doesn't understand.

The farm

1. Draw a large paddock.

2. There is a pig sty in the paddock with two pigs in it.

3. It is a sunny day.

4. A tractor is in the paddock.

5. A farmer is on the tractor.

6. There are some cows in the paddock.

18

Reading again

Read the story without any pictures.

GOING TO THE FARM

On Saturday morning Dad came into my bedroom.

"Get out of bed and put on some old clothes", said Dad. "We are going to visit a farm."

At nine o'clock we got in the car and drove to the farm.

We went through the gate and the farmer came out to meet us.

First we walked into a paddock and looked at the pigs. They were in a pig sty.

"Sometimes the pigs are out in the paddock", said the farmer, "but they come back into the pig sty for food."

We walked through the gate into another paddock. There were some sheep and a horse in the paddock.

"We get meat and wool from the sheep", said the farmer, "but the horse is a friend. Would you like to have a ride on him?"

"Yes please", I said quickly.

The farmer lifted me on to the horse. He led the horse with a rope.

I sat on the tractor and I climbed up on the hay in the hayshed. We put some hay on the back of the tractor and fed the hay to the cows.

It was a good day. We went home at four o'clock.

STORY 5: GOING SHOPPING

Vocabulary

 butter

 bread

 bananas

milk

 rice

cabbage

potatoes

 chocolate

 biscuits

sausages

oranges

shopping list

 twenty dollars

ten dollars

five dollars

two dollars

 one dollar

fifty cents

twenty cents

ten cents

supermarket

bakery

butcher

Reading and writing

Read this story. Write the word on the line beside the picture.

David and Kate were going shopping. Mum gave them $20 $10 _____
and a list of food to buy.

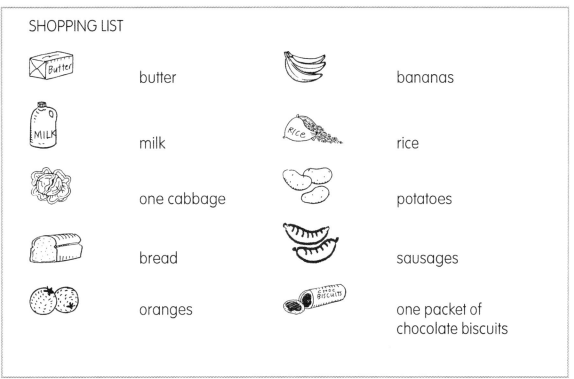

They walked to the _____ . At the _____

they bought five hundred grams of _____ Butter , some_____ ,

two litres of _____ MILK , a packet of _____ Rice , one _____ , three

kilograms of _____ , some _____ and one packet of

chocolate _____ . At the checkout the woman put their food into bags and they

paid _____ $20 $2 .

David and Kate looked at their_____ .

"We forgot the _____ ", said Kate.

"Yes", said David. "We could buy some _____ 🍞 at the _____ 🏠."

They went to the _____ 🏠 and bought one loaf of _____ 🍞. It

cost _____ ($1) and (50c) , (20c) , (10c) .

"Did we buy any sausages?" asked Kate.

"No", said David, "but we have got _____ [$5] , ($1) and (20c) left. We could go

to the _____ 🏠 and buy some sausages."

They went to the butcher's shop.

"Have you got any _____ 🌭?" asked David.

"Yes, I have some sausages", said the butcher. David paid _____ [$5] for the sausages.

When David and Kate got home, Mum said, "Did you get everything that was on the _____

_____ 📝 ?"

"Yes", said David and Kate. "We got everything and there is _____ ($1) and (20c) left

over."

"Thank you, David and Kate", said Mum.

Understanding the story

Answer the questions.

1. What did David and Kate buy at the bakery? _____

2. What did David and Kate buy at the supermarket? _____

    _____

3. What did David and Kate buy at the butcher's shop? _____

Write *Yes* or *No* on the line.

1. David and Kate went shopping._____

2. They bought some bread._____

3. They bought some fish. _____

4. They bought some apples. _____

5. They walked to the supermarket. _____

6. They had $30. _____

7. They bought some bananas. _____

8. Mum took them to the shops in the car. _____

9. They bought everything on the shopping list. _____

10. They spent all the money. _____

Naming

Write the name of the foods under the picture.

_____ _____ _____ _____ _____

_____ _____ _____ _____ _____

Sentence order

Write the words in the correct order.

1. the walked They to supermarket. _____

2. shopping. David Kate are and going _____

23

Reading again

Read the story without any pictures to help you.

GOING SHOPPING

David and Kate were going shopping. Mum gave them thirty dollars and a list of food to buy.

SHOPPING LIST	
butter	bananas
milk	rice
one cabbage	potatoes
one packet of chocolate biscuits	bread
sausages	oranges

They walked to the supermarket. At the supermarket they bought 500 grams of butter, some bananas, two litres of milk, a packet of rice, one cabbage, three kilograms of potatoes, some oranges and one packet of chocolate biscuits. At the checkout the woman put their food into bags and they paid twenty-two dollars.

David and Kate looked at their shopping list.

"We forgot the bread", said Kate.

"Yes", said David. "We could buy some bread at the bakery."

They went to the bakery and bought one loaf of bread. It cost one dollar and eighty cents.

"Did we buy any sausages?" asked Kate.

"No", said David, "but we have got six dollars and twenty cents left. We could go to the butcher and buy some sausages."

They went to the butcher's shop.

"Have you got any sausages?" asked David.

"Yes, I have some sausages", said the butcher. David paid five dollars for the sausages.

When David and Kate got home, Mum said, "Did you get everything that was on the list?"

"Yes", said David and Kate. "We got everything and there is one dollar and twenty cents left over."

"Thank you, David and Kate", said Mum.

Part 2

Meeting specific language needs

ACTIVITY 2.1: Following instructions

This activity could be used with a small group in the classroom or with individuals with a helper. Each child has a pencil and paper and a copy of the alphabet in the following layout.

A	B	C	D	E	F
G	H	I	J	K	L
M	N	O	P	Q	R
S	T	U	V	W	X
Y	Z				

A	B	C	D	E	F
G	H	I	J	K	L
M	N	O	P	Q	R
S	T	U	V	W	X
Y	Z				

A	B	C	D	E	F
G	H	I	J	K	L
M	N	O	P	Q	R
S	T	U	V	W	X
Y	Z				

One child picks up a word card (see below) and helps the others to discover the word by giving them instructions on where each letter in the word is located. For example, for the word shop, the child says:

- "Fourth line, first letter."
- Then "Second line, second letter."

These instructions continue until a child guesses the word correctly or all the letters are given.

When they have played the game using the word cards, the children could think of their own words.

car	cat	dog	big
can	shop	come	fish
bike	bird	ball	little
money	house	pencil	school
picture	teacher	mother	hamburger

ACTIVITY 2.2: Practice with prepositions

A. Fill in the gaps with the words from the box.

| on | behind | beside | on | under | in | between | in front of |

1. Some sausages and chops are _____ the barbecue.

2. _____ the barbecue is a tree.

3. A bird is up _____ the tree.

4. A table is _____ the barbecue.

5. A cat is _____ the table.

6. There are some plates and cups _____ the table.

7. Some bread is _____ the plates and cups.

8. A fruit bowl with bananas and apples is _____ the bread.

B. Answer the questions.

1. What is on the barbecue?_____

2. What is in front of the bread?_____

3. Where is the bread? _____

4. Where is the cat?_____

5. What is behind the barbecue?_____

6. Who is cooking the meat?_____

27

ACTIVITY 2.3: Ending with -ed

A. Write ed on the line.

cook_____   walk_____   talk_____   climb_____

look_____   wash _____   clean ___   kick _____

B. Write the correct word on the line. Choose from the words above.

1. She _____ the ball.

2. Dad _____ tea.

3. I _____ to my friend.

4. I _____ my hair.

5. Mum _____ the house.

6. I _____ a tree.

7. He_____ up at the plane.

8. I _____ to school.

ACTIVITY 2.4: Ending with -es

A. Read these words.

branch   box   church   brush   glass   watch

B. Write es on the line.

1. branch_____

2. box_____

3. church_____

4. watch_____

5. brush_____

6. glass_____

C. Write the correct word under the picture.

_____

_____

_____

_____

_____

_____

_____

_____

D. Read these words.

stood	spoke	wrote	came	drew	caught	ran	flew	taught	gave

E. Read these sentences.

Sometimes

I stand up.

I speak to my teacher.

I write a letter.

I come to school.

I draw a picture.

I catch the ball.

I run fast.

The bird can fly.

I give my friend a present.

I teach my little sister to play a game.

Yesterday

I stood up.

I spoke to my teacher.

I wrote a letter.

I came to school.

I drew a picture.

I caught the ball.

I ran fast.

The bird flew.

I gave my friend a present.

I taught my little sister to play a game.

F. Write the correct word on the line. Choose from the words in the box (Question D) above.

1. My teacher _____ me to read.

2. The children _____ up and went out to play.

3. I _____ a story about my holiday.

4. Mum _____ to school in the car to get me.

5. I _____ very fast.

6. I _____ the ball.

7. The pilot _____ the plane.

8. I _____ loudly to my friend.

9. I _____ the book to my teacher.

10. I _____ a picture of the playground at school.

ACTIVITY 2.5: Making more than one

A. Read these words.

mouse   mice   child   children   person   people

man   men   woman   women   tooth   teeth

foot   feet   foot

B. Write the correct word on the line. Choose from the words above (Question A).

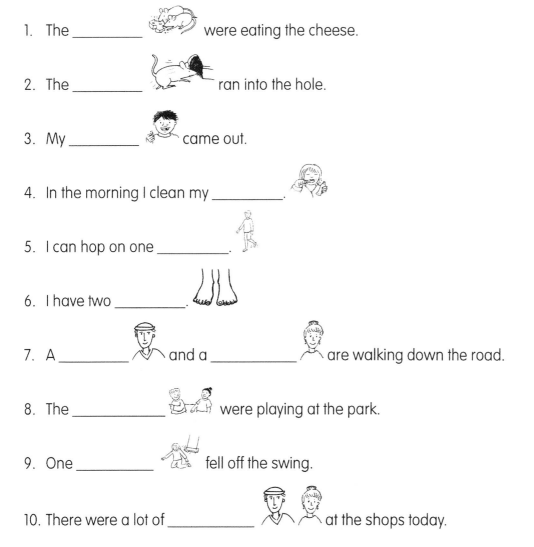

1. The _____ were eating the cheese.

2. The _____ ran into the hole.

3. My _____ came out.

4. In the morning I clean my _____.

5. I can hop on one _____.

6. I have two _____.

7. A _____ and a _____ are walking down the road.

8. The _____ were playing at the park.

9. One _____ fell off the swing.

10. There were a lot of _____ at the shops today.

31

C. Change the word so that it means "more than one".

1. mouse _____

2. tooth _____

3. foot _____

4. person _____

5. child _____

6. man _____

7. woman _____

D. Can you write the word so that it means "more than one"?

1. book _____

2. pencil _____

3. car_____

4. cat _____

5. dog _____

6. church _____

7. brush _____

8. watch _____

Part 3

Mini-focus language packs

PACK A: THE LANGUAGE OF MATHEMATICS

ACTIVITY A1: Naming basic shapes

Cut out the cards and match the shape with its name. Then find the sentences that go with each shape.

square	oblong	circle
oval	diamond	hexagon
triangle	straight line	curved line
This shape has three sides.	This shape is round.	This shape has 4 sides. Each side is the same length.
This shape has 6 sides.	This shape has 4 sides. Two sides are long and two sides are short.	This shape has 4 sides. Each side is the same length. It is not a square.

ACTIVITY A2: Remembering basic shapes

Use the cards from activity A1 for a game of Memory. Each child needs a piece of paper and something to write with.

Lay the cards out on a tray for the children to look at. After two or three minutes take the cards away. The children then write down as many shapes as they can remember, either by drawing them or by writing the names.

ACTIVITY A3: Finding shapes and objects

straight line	triangle	oblong	circle	oval	diamond	hexagon	square

top   middle   bottom   above   below   between   next to   beside

Drawing

Draw these items on the shelves.

1. Draw a ball on the top shelf.

2. Draw a cat below the ball, on the middle shelf.

3. Draw a dog beside the cat.

4. Draw a car on the bottom shelf.

5. Draw a boat beside the car.

6. Draw a book above the dog.

Matching

Cut out the cards. Match the descriptions to the diagrams.

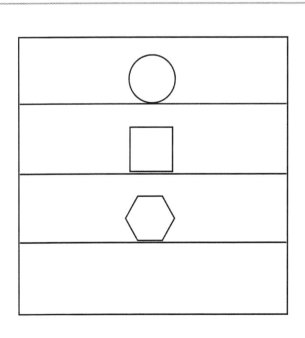
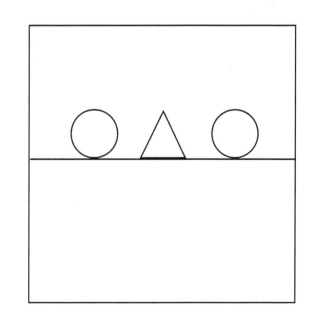

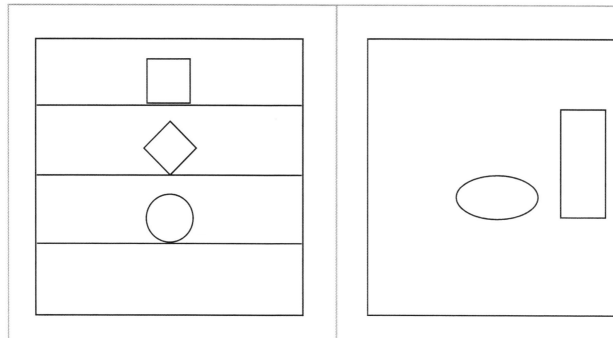

In the middle of the square is an oval. Next to the oval is an oblong.

Below the diamond is a circle. Above the diamond is a square.

There are three straight lines across the square. On the top line is a circle. On the middle line is a square. On the bottom line is a hexagon.

There is a straight line across the square. On the line are two circles. Between the circles is a triangle.

ACTIVITY A4: Working with measurements

Students need a ruler and pencil to measure and record.

measure   parallel lines   vertical lines   horizontal lines   centimetre   perimeter

Reading

Read these words.

straight line

parallel lines

curved line

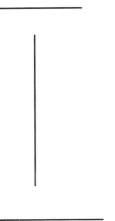

vertical line

horizontal line

This is a vertical line. It measures four centimetres.

This is a horizontal line. It measures three centimetres.

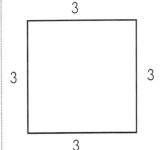

The perimeter is the distance around the outside.

3 + 3 + 3 + 3 = 12
Perimeter = 12 centimetres

1. **Measure these horizontal lines.**

2. **Measure these vertical lines.**

3. Measure the perimeters of these squares.

_____

_____

_____

_____

ACTIVITY A5: Studying symbols and words

+	−	x	÷
add	subtract	multiply	divide

=	≠	<	>
is equal to	is not equal to	is less than	is greater than

+	−	x	=
plus	minus	times	equals

Reading

Read these examples.

Add

3 + 3 = 6	three plus three equals six
5 + 4 = 9	five plus four equals nine
6 + 2 ≠ 9	six plus two is not equal to nine

Subtract

9 − 3 = 6	nine minus three equals six
10 − 4 = 6	ten minus four equals six
10 − 4 ≠ 8	ten minus four is not equal to eight

Multiply

3 x 4 = 12	three times four equals twelve
5 x 4 = 20	five times four equals twenty

Divide

20 ÷ 5 = 4	twenty divided by five equals four
18 ÷ 3 = 6	eighteen divided by three equals six

Is greater than

10 > 2	ten is greater than two
8 > 4 + 1	eight is greater than four plus one

Is less than

4 < 7	four is less than seven
2 + 4 < 10	two plus four is less than ten

Draw a line from the word to the symbol.

add   —

subtract   =

multiply   ≠

equals   +

divide   >

is not equal to   X

less than   ÷

greater than   <

Copy and cut out the words, symbols and equations. Ask the student to sort them into six groups, using these categories: **add**, **subtract**, **multiply**, **divide**, **is less than** and **is greater than**.

add	subtact	multiply	divide	plus
minus	times	is greater than	is less than	+
–	x	>	÷	<
six plus ten equals sixteen	three and three and three equals nine	ten minus five equals five	twenty minus four equals sixteen	three times seven equals twenty-one
five times four equals twenty	fifteen divided by five equals three	ten divided by two equals five	six is greater than four	ten is greater than one
five and nine and two is greater than ten	six is less than twelve	five is less than nine	4 and 7 = 11	6 + 6 = 12
10 + 10 = 20	9 – 4 = 5	20 – 4 – 6 = 10	7 minus 7 = 0	3 x 8 = 24
2 x 6 = 12	4 times 2 equals eight	16 divided by 4 = 4	9 ÷ 3 = 3	20 is greater than 10
8 > 4 + 2	7 > 6	5 is less than 9	3 + 4 < 12	11 < 18

PACK B: MY HOME

ACTIVITY B1: Household names

Draw a line to these household items.

bed   wardrobe   light   blind   computer   mirror

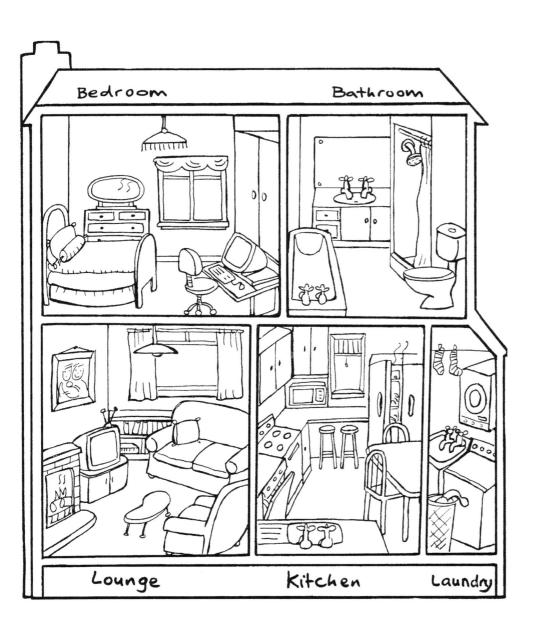

toilet

bath

shower

taps

sink

washing machine

tub

clothes basket

clothes dryer

table

stool

fridge

stove

microwave

cupboard

dishwasher

fireplace   sofa   armchair   television

picture   light   coffee table   bookshelf

ACTIVITY B2: The kitchen

Draw a picture of your kitchen at home.

Cut out the pictures, words and sentences. Mix them up so they are out of order and then match them back together.

refrigerator	sink	cupboards	microwave
table	stove	dishwasher	chair
We keep our cheese and milk in here.	We load our dirty dishes in here.	This machine cooks our food quickly.	We wash some pots in here.
I sit on this.	We keep plates and cups in here.	We put our food here when it is ready to eat.	A saucepan can cook food on this.

ACTIVITY B3: Fill the house

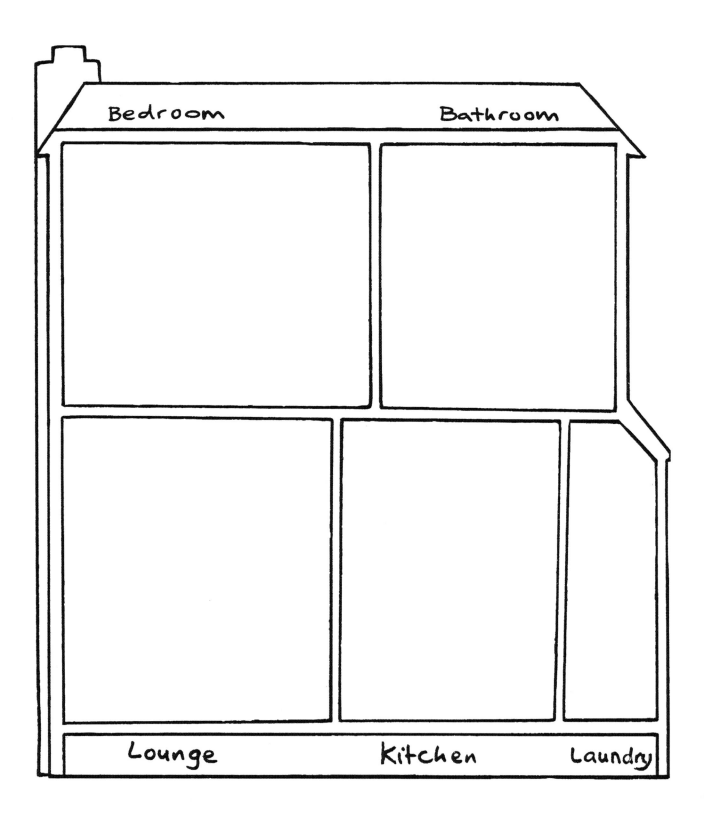

1. Write these words in the correct room.

bed   sink   toilet   television   washing machine

clothes dryer   bookshelf   dishwasher   mirror   wardrobe

tub   coffee table clothes   computer   light

bath   fridge   fireplace   sofa   clothes basket

2. Add some other household items to the rooms.

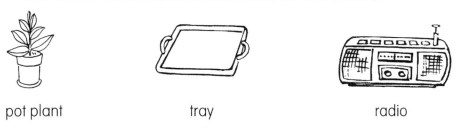

pot plant   tray   radio

broom   clock   ironing board

pillow   telephone   rubbish bin

PACK C: SPORT

THE WORLD OF SPORT: Reference page

athletics

swimming

cycling

rowing

rugby

soccer

netball

hockey

skateboarding

roller-blading

skiing

table tennis

boxing

weight-lifting

shooting

horse-riding

tennis

yachting

ACTIVITY C1: Sports at school

Name the sports equipment. Choose from these words:

hoops	large rubber balls	tennis balls	soccer ball
skipping ropes	tennis racquets	cones	whistle
hockey sticks	rugby ball	cricket bat	

_____   _____   _____   _____

_____   _____   _____   _____

_____   _____   _____

Reading

Read these sentences.

We play sport on the tennis court.

We swim in the swimming pool.

We play sport on the field.

ACTIVITY C2: Sports match

Match the words and pictures.

			athletics
			swimming
			cycling
			rowing
			rugby
			soccer
			netball
			hockey
		boxing	skateboarding
		weight-lifting	roller-blading
		shooting	skiing
		horse-riding	table tennis
		tennis	
		yachting	

ACTIVITY C3: Sports words

Write the words under the correct picture.

rugby ball	skis	netball	goal posts
hockey ball	long jump	high jump poles	roller blades
hockey sticks	shin pads	cyclist	elbow pads
racing bike	freestyle	breast-stroke	knee pads
snow	rugby field	netball court	backstroke
shotput	athletic track	cycle helmet	cycling track

_____ _____ _____ _____

_____ _____ _____ _____

ACTIVITY C4: Sports story

Cut out the pictures and the sentences. Arrange the pictures to make a story. Put the correct sentence underneath each picture.

She put on her boots and skis.	She went up the mountain on the chair lift.	She skied down the mountain.
She fell over.	She got up and brushed off the snow.	She skied to the bottom of the mountain.

PACK D: TRANSPORT

THE WORLD OF TRANSPORT: Reference page

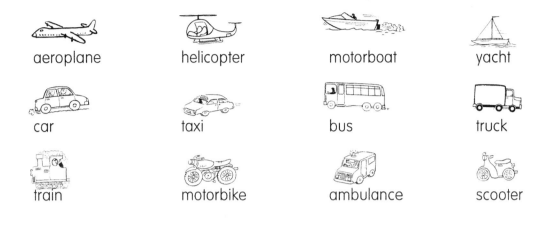

aeroplane   helicopter   motorboat   yacht

car   taxi   bus   truck

train   motorbike   ambulance   scooter

ACTIVITY D1: Going to school.

Write the missing word on the line.

1. I flew to school in a _____ .

2. I came to school on the _____ .

3. Dad drove me to school in the _____ .

4. The taxi driver drove me to school in the _____ .

5. I sailed to school in a _____ .

6. I came to school in a _____ .

7. I got a ride to school in a _____ .

8. I came to school in a _____ .

9. The ambulance driver drove me to school in an _____ .

10. I came to school on my _____ .

11. I rode to school on my _____ .

Activity D2: Naming the parts

1. Write the words in the boxes.

seat	handlebars	wheel

```
[                    ]

[                    ]

[                    ]
```

seat	steering wheel	headlight	wheel

```
[                    ]

[                    ]

[                    ]

[                    ]
```

2. Write *true* or *false* on the line.

A car has wheels. _____

A bicycle has wheels. _____

A boat has wheels. _____

An ambulance has wheels. _____

A helicopter has wheels. _____

A yacht has wheels. _____

A scooter has wheels. _____

A bus has a steering wheel. _____

A bike has a steering wheel. _____

A motorboat has a steering wheel. _____

A scooter has a steering wheel. _____

Activity D3: Bike trouble

bike

tyre

nail

Reading

Read the story.

I rode my to school. I rode over a . The went flat. I had a puncture. I walked

with my to school. My teacher rang Dad and he came to get my . After

school I walked home.

Draw the pictures in the boxes.

I rode my bike to school.	I rode over a nail.
The tyre went flat.	I walked with my bike to school.
Dad came to get my bike.	After school I walked home.